Honey Protocols

BY THE SAME AUTHOR IN ENGLISH

To Refrain from Embracing

Monika Rinck

Honey Protocols

translated from German by
Nicholas Grindell

Shearsman Books

First published in the United Kingdom in 2025 by
Shearsman Books Ltd
PO Box 4239
Swindon SN3 9FN

Shearsman Books Ltd Registered Office
30–31 St. James Place, Mangotsfield, Bristol BS16 9JB
(this address not for correspondence)

www.shearsman.com

EU AUTHORISED REPRESENTATIVE:
Lightning Source France, 1 Av. Johannes Gutenberg, 78310 Maurepas, France.
Email: compliance@lightningsource.fr

ISBN 978-1-84861-963-0

Copyright © Monika Rinck, 2012
Translations copyright © Nicholas Grindell, 2025
Musical scores composed by Bo Wiget © Bo Wiget, 2012

The rights of Monika Rinck to be identified as the author of this work,
and of Nicholas Grindell to be identified as the translator thereof
have been asserted by them in accordance with the
Copyrights, Designs and Patents Act of 1988.
All rights reserved.

ACKNOWLEDGEMENTS
Earlier versions of some of these translations appeared in *Inaesthetics, Bat City Review,
The White Review, Lyrikline.org, Loch Raven Review,* and *Modern Poetry in Translation.*
Thanks to the editors involved.

Originally published as *Honigprotokolle* by kookbooks, Berlin, in 2012.
Thanks to kookbooks for permission to publish this translation.

Contents

Translator's note — 9

Unio Weasel — 13
Honey Mockery — 14
Friedrich Nietzsche Ponders Love — 15
By Dint of a Screen — 16
Heaven's Hardness — 17
The Periodic System — 18
The Terrors and Promises of Satan — 19
Moorlands Totilas — 20
It's Fontosch — 21
Kettle Drum Surprise — 22
Peak Fogash — 23
The Arbiter's Sick — 24
Depletion Via Duplication — 25
Translation — 26
Ho Ho Hotel — 27
Completeness — 28
The Picture — 29
Spring's Coming — 30
The Lake — 31
Rhododendronrhododendron — 32
Mountain — 33
The Impossible — 34
Rabbits — 35
The Farce — 36
On Romanticism — 37

File Dividers	38
Straw	39
Eye-Tentacle Fish	40
Der Identisch	41
Tipping	42
Friendship	43
The Same	44
No Restaurants, Honey	45
Ma Dignité (Canon for Four Voices)	45
The Mistake	46
Bag with Fur	47
Deletion	48
Regret	49
Situation	50
What It Was	51
The Soufflé	52
Germs	53
Want	54
Theory of Affect	55
Round World	56
Money	57
Boozing	58
Shellfish	59
Begat	60
Kalokagathia	61
Kalokagathia (Carnival Song)	62
End-of	64
Day's Debris	65
Song of the Ingrate Party Guests	66
Gambling	70

Equilibrium	71
Fur	72
Who Who Who	73
Scent	74
Shade Plants	75
Haydn	76
Poplars	77
Solitary Sobbing	78
I Lie Down (Canon for Four Voices)	79
Atlas	80
Diva and Dealer	81
Trap	82
Hive Mind	83
Driving Permit	84
Honey	85

Translator's note

In German, the commonest meaning of *Protokoll* is *minutes*, the written record of a meeting, which fits the stickiness of honey, capturing the minutiae of what's going on, a stickiness that's also there etymologically, a protocol originally being a flyleaf glued to the outer page of a manuscript (from Greek *prōto-*, first, and *kolla*, glue). *Protokoll* also has the commonest meaning of *protocol* in English, a prescribed code of required behaviour. Because *protocol* is not generally used for minutes (even if some dictionaries do list such a meaning), my earliest translations of these poems, begun before they were published in 2012, used chronicle instead. One of these early attempts was 'Eye-Tentacle Fish', which Monika decided to include in her original book because it added something not in the German, something "found in translation". For this English version of the collection, I asked her to translate 'Eye-Tentacle Fish' back into German, and in the process she found something new that's in neither her German original, '*Augenfühlerfisch*', nor my English.

Honey Protocols

Seven sketches for poems such as are very good

UNIO WEASEL

Honey protocols! Hear how they mock? In amber & ambergris:
delightfully (or frightfully?) the weasel couples in the thicket
with the cylinder head gasket, tubes, fan belts, twitching parts.
How fleet the weasel is, how heavy the very braked car wreck
from whose leaks synthetic emulsions flow, shimmering pink.
Crazy 'twas, the protocol tells, as pines themselves did divest.
Needles dropped, arrows, dainty and fresh, barely controlled.
That's the heavens' blondest projectile – the sun? Or Sonja
with the silver rifle? Scenting stags. Birch trees mimic alternators.
Low on prey drive, a felled octahedron lifts its nose from the trail.
Ah, spare the forests, instead of stacking them with broken stuff.
For in good time, this old tub will swamp the pleasures. Recently
fit, in tender loving union with the remains of the tin roof (shed!),
now in wretched form. Derelict. Condemned. Unio Weasel Finito.

HONEY MOCKERY

Honey protocols! Hear how they mock? Golden, good and gooey.
Viscidities. Bits of fluff. What the honey binds to itself? Protocols.
Flocked amalgams on grey to blue-grey jersey material. People.
Will. Get. Stuck. Seeds and pollen likewise. Airborne sweetness.
Candied hair, lengths of it. Bridges. If I spike it up on my head
it stands on end forever. Every measure's true in every sense.
But in relation to what? All these leaps! Baroque minimizer
of longing. Wild diversity, a thousand and one things folded in,
but not put into practice. Now it's growing right out of my skin,
no longer beneath it. Baroque. In plight, fright, carrion, no: clarion,
so much adornment that you want no more, can no longer see:
Oh for an edge! Myriad arches. With dings and cherubs. Beading.
Et encore. Every woman asks: And you still think you want to?
No. What you tell them's no. Your impression's no sure fit for truth,
notes the honey protocol, sweetness adorned. Did your tongue
go over the brim? Did it tip the scales? Take fresh measure,
with minimized longing. You know nothing of the Baroque. Pollen.

FRIEDRICH NIETZSCHE PONDERS LOVE

Honey protocols! Hear how they mock? Snow white and super blue:
On the footpaths, we are told, radiators grapple with hydrants and
at the marble quarry puss licks her belly until the shag is fluffed.
Get well cards addressed to third parties. The cable car's driving
crank whirs. Here dwells Friedrich Nietzsche. On ukulele, recording
his propaedeutics in song. Huzza, a subcutaneous Alpine ditty.
Dissimilarity as a religious doctrine. The root chord: E minor.
Robert Walser says Friedrich Nietzsche was not. Huh? What?
What was I not? You were not loved. Hence your resentment.
The vengeful perfidy of one unloved. Meanwhile, new arrivals tuck
in to hearty snacks. Sausage. Berries. Poire Williams and Gentian.
Friedrich Nietzsche and the gentle master of remorse converse
on stacking chairs. Are they onions? Are those contacts – or blows
with the fan? Is it a hand-forged bark spud, swathed in camellia oil?
We don't know. They speak quietly. The mountains' endless murmur.
Friedrich Nietzsche ponders love. Robert Walser smiles in silence.

BY DINT OF A SCREEN

Honey protocols! Hear how they mock? Hair, hours, greed,
fireballs, the dump was ablaze. Space weapons plummeted,
unchecked, like icing sugar into hotels with indoor pools. I saw
the stud farms in the lowlands fall prey to random marauders,
or was it the waning health of a winch? Do something! By dint
of a screen! Lower it. Stare blinkingly into the asymptote.
I saw embers burn out, saw them expire and slowly disperse,
I saw animals milking themselves. Saw how they strained
something through a sieve. Round yards circled, a panicked herd
broke right through the middle of a giant pincushion. Reeds! I saw
the whipped flush in the cheeks of the tenors, I saw gangsters,
verdigris, mixed terrain, mimesis. Wickerwork was the arms trade
of a language family. Superior drug runners I saw partaking
of grilled fare and Peking vegetables. I saw, running their errands
in compliant impotence, chess hostesses, gramps, ushers.
I cast my eyes heavenwards. There were big birds up there, tracing
their lines. Heavens there were, even where usually: murder.

HEAVEN'S HARDNESS

Honey protocols! Hear how they mock? A dusky demi-monde.
Is it air or wall? Mute birds, decoy throstles, nay sparrows,
cast in resin and hardener, captured in see-through cubes.
Enough to make you cry. Or chirrup and hop in lieu of bird.
But for now a heavy sleep lies over you and only your dream
knows of the others. It thinks for you. As in: What's a rack?
To purposefully place something inside, with sure swift hand.
Because it belongs there, an affront, such a good fit, you shiver.
Now you lie awake in your tent of cash, you want to foot the bill.
Stay here, wait for the end of the wall. Adorn the day's edges
with slumber, no, worse still, plait this kitsch into your locks.
But hey, vulnerable life in the morning, surely that's not nothing!
No wrong word, get up and see, out the window, how a dusky
demi-monde dawns, look! An orange-tip lands, quivers, explodes.

THE PERIODIC SYSTEM

Honey protocols! Hear how they mock? Beastly super-beings zap,
ha ha! Get them to tell you whom they mock. The defenseless ones,
people lying under continental quilts, sleeping, knowing nothing
of each other whatsoever. Is the early morning air not too heavy
to breathe? You're awake, remember: there's metals in your lung.
On starched sheets of sky, guilt becomes a question, or a clock.
Show something, in eyeshot, send someone, to fetch stuff, please:
if you go to the kiosk, bring Schnitzler and celeriac. That's to say:
tobacco and vodka. A day that's aging at such immense speed, but
having no age yet oneself. Hear the clatter of those who've risen, out
there on the ledge of the morning. You want fondue for breakfast?
Deep-fried eggs? The Tartarean trio of haggis, black pud'n'turnips?
No, no, no, no pain is what we want to have. We want lines of grout
bigger than the tiles. And for a needless end we've less stomach still.

THE TERRORS AND PROMISES OF SATAN

Honey protocols! Hear how they mock? Words being used:
Earth's guts and Devil's visage, import, export, gnosis, bosom.
The gods protrude into the unfamiliar world and become evil.
That's un-Ancient. That's prittle-prattle in the profound sense.
Disinfernalization subcontracted. Outsource the diabolic share,
that's how gnosis operates. It separates the one from the other.
The guise is creaturely like the body of the Devil, bat sleeves,
pitch-black sequins. Everyone procures and wears it alone,
but wears it for all. Import was the Fall, export was redemption.
The text speaks of de-Tartarization and means redistribution.
Separative accumulation as the world's end and, so to speak,
its salvation. For sure. Let no one believe he or she can enter
Earth's guts with impunity. Let no one say their bosom is pure.
Those were the words: Earth's guts and Devil's visage, plus
import, export, gnosis, bosom. And that's how they're used.

MOORLANDS TOTILAS

Honey protocols! Hear how they mock? Black, gleaming, trained.
The beast does what you want and does it well, so well you almost
believe it wants it itself – how you want it's what it, too, wants.
We suspect it of pride. But will it ever be able to take on board
all the excitement it unleashes? A performance, almost sexual and
sometimes just as twisted, the ecstasy of tension or an intimate
bond between ruler and ruled. Even the strongest animal is
endlessly moronic. Says who? Adorno. Heels sprung, knees high,
pirouettes, transitions down at the gallop, insane shoulder machine.
A sea otter on a tight rein! As if nature were just one element among
others and could be switched, like a vehicle that goes on dry land
but that also goes on water, and then in the end it can even fly.
As if a horse were to fly through the sky! So please help it land.
Horses land best in jelly desserts that have yet to fully curdle,
in unset blancmange. Or they break into a gallop as they come in
to land, then hit the ground running and gallop on unscathed…

IT'S FONTOSCH

Honey protocols! Hear how they mock? So deep in the South it makes
the South vomit. The summer dress retrieved from the puke at dawn.
A morning of tears, then lunchtime distress – as if brightness itself
were falling to the ground, never to get up again. The alarmed hairs
in the small of the back. We speak not, but we know not whereof. Food.
Leftover food. Then parlour games. The game's called: Forest Porter.
One player decides, the others wear a lichen's or a pine's disguise.
A player is chosen to exit, enter – or do nothing at all. There are rules
about beavers and curtains. As a beaver, you fashion your territory.
As a curtain, you keep your territory covered. What'll you be? *It's fontosh.*
Make up your mind. Faster, *it's peak fontosh*. But then again you could
throw an eight, which would mean you're in store for the bones. These
you'll keep, along with the liquefied bikini (shame's Hegel) as a joker,
though it'll cost you. You'll need more than twelve lime-green doodads,
and peach fuzz round your mouth, a mouth fit for kissing, over and over.
Whether you win will depend on how many doodads you have in reserve.
Did it ever cross your mind that hope has put you on the wrong track,
chastening you to the ground? If so you're out, unless you sing farewell
a hundred times while taking leave, in which case you're back in the game.

KETTLE DRUM SURPRISE

Honey protocols! Hear how they mock: You don't want that.
Doesn't the space become a cathedral? An all-male spa?
Or a Lutherus? I delight to do your will. But get this straight:
bandages look beautiful, very beautiful, on beautiful people.
That says nothing about the bandages. Neither does it tell us
how tightly they're wound, if not to say bound. Nor does it say
wherefore. The image is crude or undue. Remove it. Everything
might fall apart, might perish. Or, on the contrary, it might all
make a permanent recovery. Unlike the business of perishing,
recovering depends on relatedness. That alone enables it.
To do what though? Think. Well, you have no words, but what you
have no words for you want to possess. Steel on steel-blue sky,
a handle, to put something in or fetch something out, a rack,
a very big hand full of plums. What would that be in English?
In plain English one would say: a most devoted kettle-drummer.

PEAK FOGASH

Honey protocols! Hear how they mock: It's fogash, darling,
peak fogash, and springtime too. You know what you see?
You're a danger, or: You're in danger (as you wish.) Stumble!
Stumble blindly into the paternoster that rises to meet your fall.
That was a near thing. Say thank you. You were spared.
Sometimes it's said that people with very poor eyesight have
such faculties, that their eyes are like ties, bound to the other,
unable to tear themselves away from a view they can't even see.
That they're most amiable towards they're not quite sure whom.
And curvature's augmented and peripheral retardation's greater,
or it's best to circumvent a border, after all they don't know
where it's at. With rather shy hands that grasp only once
they're sure they're where the handle is, then linger. Linger on.

THE ARBITER'S SICK

Honey protocols! Hear how they mock? I'm still asleep,
they're fighting already. My assistants are whacking each other
with hangers and brushes. Oh boy, the arbiter's sick today.
I see how they batter their limbs, whose workforce is mine,
in order, thus squandered, to own themselves at long last.
Or so the assistants think. How wrong they are! Whizz bang,
the ankle joint, the nose bone. Cat's tongue, mop and deerfoot.
OMG. Who'll sew this for me? Who'll stitch it up? Who'll fetch
and bring back, who'll support, who'll transcribe? What do
mops and moping have to do with each other? Check it for me!
Enough of the fisticuffs! When do we go to print? Assistants,
get to work! The theme is: The arbiter's sick today. Let's go!
Mixed dactyls, skipping rhythms, inner universe of middle rhyme.
Bear me forth and write it all down. Realize me in places
where I cannot set foot. And, while conciliation soon prevails,
it's still lying there, the cuddly toy of my tattooed assistant,
who always was my favourite. Ah! I'll never sack a single one.

DEPLETION VIA DUPLICATION

Honey protocols! Hear how they mock? They mock your cares.
I'm racked with cares. They mock your tendon. *I'm so high-strung.*
They watch your ankles, through your shoes. You're well sorted,
not at all overstretched. But addiction's this tipping over forwards –
sustained anxiety. Haggling over concepts. Caulking over talking.
The man at the railing wants to know: What's true, what's not?
A tipping. Salvage. Or rather self-salvage. At least the shoes.
Your standing's no good. It's your ankles. Draw back the cares,
the longing, and let them fly. Have an outstanding standing.
Then wait. Await the return of cares. And while you're waiting
never shift from the spot. Display steady signs of neglect.
Let yourself inertly go. Silt up. Give quarter to parasites.
And then, lastly, take the mockery and wash. Wash your shirts.
Wash your trousers and hair in mockery, too. Later, cleansed,
continue longing. Stand amidst your cares. Be your own mockery.

TRANSLATION

Honey protocols! Hear how they mock? You translated yourself –
didn't you? – into everything. You translated your shirtsleeves,
your crumbs, right on into The Great Glory, where they vanished
instead of helping, or hampering. You stared up into The Glory,
you leaped up at it, but the force of your leap was too feeble
for your heaviness. Gadzooks. Glory can be reached by express
train in roughly ten seconds, but not by you. Everybody knows
you were mistaken. It said *elephant flap* and you translated it as
waggly tail. And when dates were proffered to the welcome guest
what was it you wrote down? *Please demolish the rendezvous.*
Ready you was, good you wasn't, this you knew, you was muddled.
Cloud-sized losses, so nothing serious, launched into distance
and getting lighter: then many many realizations at vanishing point.

HO HO HOTEL

Honey protocols! Hear how they mock? Ho ho, they send you
to an airport hotel! They say: Go where it's ugly, and pricey,
and choose the wrong bed, but don't sleep in it, just lie there,
and as you lie there, hear how artfully the air to tatters is torn
by the propeller-driven planes that are forever taking off,
forever landing, forever to tatters tearing. Get a good rest.
From how many thousand feet up? No! Not that, please.
You're not to be one more booster of the void. Be peculiar.
But what for? You must outlast, overwinter into the old rage,
into the willingness to make something worse. Not to barter
but to smash. When they say: or vice versa for a change,
what do you say? You say: NO. Impressionism's over, finito.
Look, all the others, who were promiscuous but pure of heart,
are going away. *Away*? But you've already been there!
How much is that in dollars, sex, or hours? Stop, cut it out,
no more bartering. Tomorrow you'll be off on your travels
and you'll tell them all: It's more than any of you can afford.

COMPLETENESS

Honey protocols! Hear how they mock? There, on Lychener Straße,
at three in the morning, we're told, it was like a frisson: completeness.
This we owe to The Horse Woman and for this, as of today, we like her.
It was light in the dark, we're told, sparks of eyelashes, rain of sparks
from above, or rather from below, like standing over a golden fountain,
a mighty indoor firework, and dancing on the table, something I can't do
of course (!) but something I could somehow do inwardly, light broken
down, dissolved into sets, vectors and weightless volumes, dismantling
before my eyes, there was the face, in the shimmer a regrouping of lips,
lids, effervescent lines, teeth and temples! Eternity's duration was roughly
90 seconds, three in the morning, then Remo had to go, and it was over.

THE PICTURE

Honey protocols! Hear how they mock? They've got an eye on you. Follow their gaze, don't budge. The room and all the people in it flattened to a picture and traced through with thinners, mimeoed, hung up again in the same place. And: What are you looking at? Is Remo still in it? We're here, in the place where hot eyes see what anxiety cools back down again. Polar lighting. Freeze-frame, opportunity not taken. *Femme futile,* forsaken. What'll you do? Take the picture and walk away. You can't do what tempts you, you can't do it. Just believe me. I'm picturing it clearly for you. But is the most wretched of sinners not he who finds sinning's beyond his capacities? No. It's a kind person with your eyes and big wishes, who desires and ends up going home with the picture.

SPRING'S COMING

Honey protocols! Hear how they mock? One Spring always imitates
the next, always menacing like some guy who says he'll join us
at the restaurant later, prompting us to spirit away the knives,
otherwise Spring'll make us new, or whatever it thinks that might be,
frantically basting time, everting everything, to see how it looks
when the inside's turned out, if everything's then been said at last.
Spring's coming, wants to expand us, enlarge us endlessly, scatter us
(please get rid of the knives, tell the waiters, too) in open country,
the enchantment of the veins, Spring passes through with blossoms,
with the imaginings of blossoms to come, hibiscus! Spring will come,
it'll tear us apart in blue skies, and we'd burn to a cinder in blossoms
of future indifference. Oh you bundled neurons, you stubborn winters
and clocks, set yourselves to twelve, greet it, the Spring: here it comes.

THE LAKE

Honey protocols! Hear how they mock? These two young men
sailed out onto the lake on a trampoline. It had a springy deck
that bore their weight, three masts and yes, the masts lifted and
flipped the thing up at the corners and no, they didn't go overboard.
First I saw all this from below, and I was an alga. Then I saw it
hachured from the side, and I was reeds. Later, when I was sky,
I saw them both from above. They groped their way swiftly forward,
seemed to have a theme. But then I saw them capsize and sink!
The lake took the trampoline to heart. When that happened I was
the shore. I swear, I was never the lake! What was I meant to do?
I became the bottom and burrowed my way in. Then I bounced back,
almost like a trampoline, yes, and spat the two of them in a high arc
onto the promenade. The lake came to, converged in me once more.
The reeds alone, nothing else, moved. Overhead, the sky was calm.

RHODODENDRONRHODODENDRON

Honey protocols! Hear how they mock? Pipe down already
you dope. But what if I said no to the structural logic of lack?
You'd need some frank words. And you'd have to schlepp,
pluckable ripeness, woven, shoved to the top of the slide,
every last little detail, electrified, the status indicator lights
on your instinct's transformer all aflicker, on, off, on, off,
on, on, on, on. You'd also have to get closer, to be gondola,
tongs and lobster. Parasite attack. Hirsuteness on hands,
on bonnets, cowlings and marble. But then, at some point,
you'd also have to slide down. How do you think it'd look,
the rhododendron, after this slippery exercise? Precisely.
Who'd dare to rollick in the old growth at the Wörlitz-Dessau
Garden Realm? And how'd they be left looking? Self-denial
is common to dandies, pensioners and ascetics. But only
the dandy would contemplate a demolition. You're inhibited,
it's true. Wait a minute! I'm not inhibited!!! That, too, is true.

MOUNTAIN

To begin with, some Wittgenstein: language, thought, limits, etc..
A near superhuman endeavour, to describe using language,
when thinking doesn't come, yes, dear protocols, you lag behind
the mocking scorn I've long aimed at myself, voilà. And anyhow:
I imagine it as a mountain. Describe mountain. Maybe three lines.
Then evasive manoeuvre. Protestant dialectics. Fluent, sharp.
Nimble. Malicious, but souped up: HA HA. Overtone of despair.
And now: enter wigged roebuck. Aah. Compassion. Slight disgust.
Oho! Red herring: short-term absolution, hint of relaxation, only
to snap fiercely into the latch as soon as the tension subsides,
like with a karabiner, clack. Next up: words of welcome and razing
the mountain, with power shovels and brandy, 200-dB symphonies
by Haydn, with lengthy movements blasted out, with compressed air,
with crowbars and gelignite and a whole host of heavy equipment.
The mountain says: all will soon be level and clear. Then start over.

THE IMPOSSIBLE

The impossible is – you want to know what? Pah! How the lecture was? The one he can only recall if twelve beers are set before him at once, by a snippersnapper of a waiter who so wishes he were something other than what he is that we should give him a good sound thrashing. Then, refreshed by gratitude, he'd recall what he's capable of and what not. Don't laugh, it starts off small, a stimulus can build and grow endlessly, but a mindset sadly cannot! The slightest thing can be impossible, but the mightiest might be too. The impossible reframes the references. And I don't even have to pay. The lecture was good, he said. Philosophy penetrated the oeuvre's most sensitive surfaces at burned-out spots, added to which, apparently, generation is quasi-unleavable. I'm afraid that was as much as I could get out of my brother. He wasn't drunk enough to recall the whole thing verbatim. The impossible: that which – no one can do. That's the democratic aspect. Those who crow about it can't do it either, but believe themselves complicit with it and speak, for example, of an impossible start, as if they were intimately acquainted. Put it this way: Whoever posits as impossible what passes for impossible has never given it a try. Freeze. Freeze, for the godhead's got a cough.

RABBITS

Honey protocols! Hear how they mock? With room-filling voices,
but without me seeing the room they fill. I'm in the hypnosis tent.
A gentle draught, trembling wavering lengths that soon fall still
from top to bottom once more, like opaque colours, orange,
with a voice passing through, interconnecting the sections.
It tells me what I am: I'm relaxed. Thus I lie alone in sound
and listen, I'm a pack of rabbits that have stopped scurrying.
Intervening in the soul's dynamics: what's associated, inhibit,
and what's lately dissociated, re-associate. Changing cubicle.
But what do I clandestinely shed, what comes loose or snags?
Since images are not able to pass unharmed like a voice
through the pores of things, I'm blind rabbits, we're relaxed.
Meanwhile, the hypnotist in laddered lace stockings mumbles
as he stumbles on the deep shag pile between the cubicles.
Black-barked thighs, as if something were crawling concertedly
over them, like a voiced Z, buzzing, textured. I think: rabbits.
I'm relaxed, I have failed. Rabbits, rabbits, always rabbits.

THE FARCE

Honey protocols! Hear how they mock? Recording all that
takes place and restaging it, or at least pretending that's what
they'll do, like the farce that amused Constantin Constantius
so mightily that he lay in his first balcony box, tossed away
like the clothes of a bather, floored and convulsed, beside
the torrents of laughter. This he wished to repeat, of course,
and he suffered a failing less of the protocol than of this world,
which cares little for convulsive boxes, while the venerable
Herr Kafka, in the same box with his wife, busied himself
feverishly with the lady's little knife, trying his damnedest
to excise from the balustrade's padding a rival, *Come to me,
sweet mistress*, a long thin man sewn into the velvet upholstery
as an admirer, and throw him into the stalls, which didn't work
out either, or we know nothing of it. Here, the protocol failed.

ON ROMANTICISM

Honey protocols! Hear how they mock? It's them woebegone songs, collapse and then stay put, just so, ideally right in front of a door that opens outwards, so that somebody leaving won't go unnoticed. Something I can welcome, simpering felicity, that's the thing, right? Pure affirmation. But – some of them I must penalize nonetheless, because of asymmetry, I'm just saying. In the harem of mildness I'm the strictest. Crown is cypress wreath. And harp may be murder axe. Everyone's blasted into outer space. Anyone rushing into a squeeze like that'll marvel, looking back, at where he or she is, in comparison. Listen up, I'll say this just the once: If you have a friend here below do not trust him at this hour. And if you must mindlessly fling yourself into the funnel, make sure it's the latest funnel, where the canon can't strike a second time because it's been shifted by its own affect, be it by a mere hair's breadth. I crawl. Romanticism. Overwhelming that I can welcome. Too late for you, you've understood. Wood. Wood.

FILE DIVIDERS

Honey protocols! Hear how they mock? A pixilated roundelay of mine own words (spun to your timeless honor and grace) did I perform for you, for hours, forsaken by sense. But I see you tired with heavy, outsize feet. Seeking something, like peace perhaps, the sleepy seed, perchance to germinate? Or your bare hands, molting needles. The fir house. Go on in, on into the dusty thicket, down it breaks. Hair thine. Hair mine. Sleep fine. In the dream, cooked avocados, ffs. Was assistant to an experienced prostitute. She worked bureaus, in halls and corridors, men were sometimes quite vile to her. Using cardboard (file dividers!) we made replicas of vulvas, inside them claggy residues. Probably a fetish, but one that makes sense? Wonders … yours truly and says: Good night. We'll be repeating the whole thing tomorrow. So you've still got time.

STRAW

Honey protocols! Hear how they mock? Sensitivity has now
expanded, now it's straddled and set fire to each and every space.
Earthly sadness, a greying of birch trees, an eye the dog has lost.
Ash, flaky dithering, atonement, fatigue, grief perhaps, but your duty
is to walk on through, as if it's light where misery stands, with hands
you conceive of as bound. Then you see: your grasp is dwindling.
Clarity can now be had only with a drastic shock. A soundless bang.
Your grip has gone, you're jittery, and trying to grasp nonetheless
you come right out again on the other side, relief that doesn't exist,
tremolo that doesn't exist, as if you'd just reached out into the fog,
got saddled with a foggy little horse (giddy gee, the grey's thrown me,
I'm falling through him) and you're down deep, sensitive, ungrasped,
awaiting the shock. But suddenly, here, it's all yellow, full of straw!

EYE-TENTACLE FISH

Honey protocols! Hear how they mock? It's far from certain that what's clear's always light; could just as well be darkened by elucidation, while forfeiting none of: what's already clear. The way it is for fishes. That can see the difference, but not express it. The eye-tentacle fish, for instance, that's blind to its own doodad. But who amongst us escapes this fate? With the eye-tentacle fish, though, doodad's not blind to fish. By using its outboard eye, it distinguishes precisely between what's clear but dark and what's dark and unclear to boot. With its eye-arm, the built-on telescope, it sees this clearly. Look, an eye-tentacle fish disguised as an algae-clad pebble. Madly lit, far too bright. With this eye, it sees only what's dark, with the other eye it sees itself, if it's light. With both, it sees what's clear flaring up in the dark, but because it's in disguise it doesn't see itself. And one more thing: water shouldn't burn.

DER IDENTISCH

Honigprotokolle! Hörts wie sie höhnen! Es ist ja alles andere
als gewiss, dass das Klare immer auch hell ist, es könnte
ja ebenso gut durch Darlegung nachdunkeln, ohne an Klarheit
zu verlieren. Wie es für Tische ist. Die den Unterschied sehen,
aber nicht ausdrücken können. Bspw. für den Identisch, der blind
für den eigenen Nuppsi ist. Doch wer von uns wäre das nicht?
Wobei beim Identisch der Nuppsi nicht blind für den Tisch.
Durch sein Außenauge unterscheidet er genau, was klar, doch dunkel,
vom dem, was dunkel und zudem unklar ist. Mit seinem Augen-Arm,
dem eingebauten Teleskop, kann der Identisch das genau sehen.
Schau, ein Identisch getarnt als veralgtes Rüschengemisch.
Irre erhellt, viel zu grell. Mit diesem Auge sieht er nur was dunkel,
mit dem anderen nur sich selbst, falls hell. Mit beiden sieht er
was klar aufblitzt im Dunkeln, aber da er ja verkleidet ist,
sieht er sich selber nicht. Und: Wasser soll löschen, nicht brennen.

TIPPING

Honey protocols! Hear how they shittle? Whisper, to tipping point.
Question for the protocol: What's meant by tipping here? Perhaps
whatever just bulldozed the concept? Broke it down into misfortune,
irredeemable wabbit jokes, smoke. Now we await the inner freeze,
where there's no difference between stir and don't move a muscle.
Ears down, press yourself into a hollow, listen hard. It gets heavy,
as if you were dragging something around that's no longer yourself.
That talks. That fights. That wants to choke you with your shoulders.
There's something inside you that hates you no end. It stands there.
It leaves nothing unused. Want to check the script? From the outset
everything's written down. When leaving the house becomes identical
with standstill in the yard, because yard is the same as keep walking,
no difference to be seen, unscathed and at the same time shattered,
still not tired but tired of everything else. Most interesting: your eyes
have stopped blinking. Everything goes right past them, uninterrupted.

FRIENDSHIP

Other functions we observe. Other switcheroos. Imagine a shared space of attentiveness, to be entered not alone but solely in the company of a he-friend or a she-friend. Few are so designed that three can breeze about inside. Many are stricter on this twoness than the couple space. But not really. He-friend or she-friend would never dare, never want, to tie the space shut. Mirrors don't show this. Out of respect for the friendship, he-friend or she-friend may fall in love with false, evil, weak and stupid people, this isn't prevented, but chaperoned. Shared. Friendship is more precious than that, for in friendship, unlike in love, indifference can never become proof of trust. Or closeness surreptitiously arise from bad treatment. Mimetic desire's regulated by participation. In Slovenian this takes the dual.

THE SAME

Honey protocols! Hear how they mock: This is yet more of the same!
No, no, no, say I, raising objection. But the Delphic engineers proclaim:
As per the terms and conditions of your sojourn on this dented planet,
you must try for at least a little bit of contrast. But I am trying, really I…
Yeah right, say the engineers. How am I… The engineers say nothing.
Hold on, that's preposterous, if I, which isn't even possible, wanted to
describe again and again and then, potentially, finally, even realize, or
worse still, if this wanting was…! Couldn't care less, say the engineers.
You've not used up all the words yet. Where's the list? Under the poplar,
buried. Unearth it! In a Siberian downdraft the greenfinch fidgets,
in the salty water dolphins galore play rogue wave; with help from belts
they flood the bull's-eye, Babylon! Rocket flares light up the eighties,
harbourmaster's amazed, steps out of his cubbyhole, avert your gaze!
The sirens howl. Anyone who owns a veil will surely make use of it now.
Oh please, please, leave me alone already. This is yet more of the same!
All just another load of old Delphi or what? That won't do. Use your brain.

NO RESTAURANTS, HONEY

Honey protocols! Hear how they mock? They target your shame.
Tricksters, cheerfulness of thought, of the kind ascetics require.
Abyss of eternal guilt, which is also gratitude; humility and vanity
come together when you love people so much that you – *STOP!*
Scratch that. Begin with details, then establish positions. *À bas
le SPOOK.* I want to see what you see. Don't see it. Don't dare.
HANTÉ(e). Shame on you, *à ma place*, sharing the site of shame.
And in Dijon, as she walked past, a woman in high heels said
(I swear it's true): *J'ai gardé ma dignité, j'ai* épousé *un chien.*
Praise the disengaged! In the atomic age, we're all – *ARRÊTE!*
I kill off, chop off the worms, the wires, the hoses (of the heart)
on which the resurrected are strung up, transported, moved.
Now it gets hard, very, sorry. That was the limit. *No restaurants
beyond this line, honey.* Which matters not at all, for then we'll be
like cherubim and no longer belong to anyone. Be hard-handed
cherubs, *ni femme, ni homme,* no longer belong to anyone, *enfin.*

MA DIGNITÉ (canon for four voices)

THE MISTAKE

Erreur, terreur. The whole time, I was just deleting the index system.
The stuff itself is all still there, but no one knows whereabouts. It'll be
steeping somewhere down below in the watery punch. Wan Boëthius,
hirsute. Lakeland lady, flower of the plain, lint-free whoring, meaning:
three things. For starters the file tree, minus discount, the touchphone,
plus the panels, jutting sideways into the room: *Let Nylons Be Nylons!*
And tell me why the wires now suck. The wires were meant to nourish.
Avec adoration tu peux parler autrement, so spoke French colleague,
at least that's how I understood it: worship can change your language.
Ton erreur is more than grammatical. It's fiscal. It's going to cost you,
like yoghurt. Billions. Bilious buildings. Mansplaying. *Quelle infamie!*
Then, broken midst elements free and pure, you notice: the reference
referred not least to you; more than a mere path, it was a conveyance.
It placed you in relation. Something that's now being dealt with by rocks.
A landslide doesn't refer to you, even if you were to stand against it.
Like tears shall I flow, flow till I'm hard, and hard shall I then remain.
And to demand now *il faut: dire le vrai sur le vrai,* would be something
like a session of Thai massage with Lacan – in his five-minute phase!

BAG WITH FUR

This one here is a protocol for those who are my age. This is honey for *old people*. (For now, though, note: you're as young as your bag.) You got black bag and trimmed with fur and you rummage in it, in an animal. *Chiave*, you say, *je cherche les clés. You come with me, in my macchina.* You look good and I come, in your machine. Go on, rummage in your bag like in an animal. Beautiful women here. Who smoke. Ponchos. High, swift shoes. *Mais je me demande* why you women haven't *déjà* POW! Putsch! By withholding *les devoirs du mariage, comme dans Lysistrate, par exemple? Hein?* Cry, scream, wail, scratch, hyperventilate and swoon. No, better to drive a really hard bargain. 18 hours non-stop. Then do the lightning trick, with your eyes. Nail them. *Mais tu es jeune. Très jaune. Non, non.* Was. I'm not any more. *Pour* sorting out *thighs*, you'd need to breed demigods in there. Like in a surrogate womb, a forcing leg. Kapeesh: *Demi-Dieux!* It's over. Where's the furry bag woman? In the shade of the bag she rummages in an animal. Inside it: the moon, the void, *entier*.

DELETION

Honey protocols! Hear how they mock? On the trail of
the horns, wanting to fold fire, delete it. Make it go out.
Wow, look, the twilight. The paintbrush dipped in deeply.
Aquamarine. And Payne's grey. The sprites were off to bed.
On their way home. New Moon appeared, then a Big Crack.
In the plot, the image, all of it. Inchworms at body's borders.
Was it just now, yesterday, this morning, when the woman
threw the softball? When there was no shadow and her arms
glowed red? Burned? When were the garlands? Ding dong.
When the mini dragon darted its tongue, viper style, and
there was no more fire anywhere? Remove ring from finger:
a tan line or a pencil drawing? Instances of incompleteness.
And the Big Jolt left by the Crack, and the deletion, framed
by a half-deleted scare that something's missing, but what?

REGRET

Honey protocols! Hear how they mock? Here's a suggestion:
Better to do it right now and do it quick. Then you have more
time to regret it. How will you go about it? I know how I'd do it.
I'm not telling. Hey, this could actually go even quicker still.
Are you old? Just asking. Mocking you. Far be it. Look here,
this little cup for example. Shrink-wrapped. Anyone here got
a knife? Or a bit of wire? Does anyone here among us have
a sense that things are going forwards? To our advantage?
Dream on darling! Forget it! I'm going to invent an attorney
who'll put a stop to it, so there. I'm going to invent an attorney
who'll hang himself in your lobby, explode, go up in flames.
What do you want in it? Wayawaninnit, swywonono. In the cup.
The shrunk one. You want to hesitate some more. Fine, hesitate.
We've got time. Of course we haven't! Anyone in your group still
wants to hesitate, please prepare to regret what doesn't happen.

SITUATION

Honey protocols! Hear how they mock: Analysis can also be stupor.
If that's the case, what's stupor? Stupor is sedation by concepts.
So I would say: coherence here's a fetish, a curse even. We don't
want it no more. What's curse? Negative chosenness, the opposite
of blessing. What's blessing? Blessing is, oh, think it up yourselves.
Beyond convention there's no place for deference. Completely wrong!
So what's wrong? Wrong's when one's blinded to the situation by tears
and the other sees the situation not at all. Driven to where, ultimately,
when the crash came, not even a wall. *Holding,* brow, hair. *Que faire?*
Delight yourself! No light. Oh how cheap concepts are, how sleek,
and when they're fine they're fine like wire, like a wire that cuts,
thin slices of a thing that are no longer any good to anyone at all.
No script's laid out for me here. That's clear. Beyond convention
everything must be recalculated, including decency, even grounds.
What's grounds? Grounds is the thin surface everything rests on and
breaks through. And what does that make decency? Oh, give me a break.
The situation is messy. Shouldn't the analysis be, too, to be any good?
Solve et coagula! No. It can only be dissolved very slowly, in time.

WHAT IT WAS

Honey protocols! Hear how they mock: The opposite of archaeology, they say, is irradiation; while archaeology makes prehistory accessible, they say, we lock the times to come in a blinding light. This is not true. In a frenzied state I ate steak tartare. You were the light of my eyes. Psychopharmaceuticals. And in the Italian Alps I was words written on the gas station wall, seen from a passing car. Imagine: knowing that the future can no longer be accessed – when it's not even ours. You were there, you even smoked! A glass of eau de cologne, please. The world went in, through my eyes, and came together in behind. You were there, too. But were you there really? Was it you I saw? I saw the cat, swaddled as a mummy. I saw the statue of a saint, she was reading. The avant-garde's museumification, I read, is irreversible, as apocalyptically the museum imploded into a world without people I sensed: the survival of things, the sexy undergarments of abstraction. Which means: abstraction is not an adequate answer to unimaginability. Oh you pale blue, transparent world. I saw you rush out of the shop. I saw you moving away from me. I saw Lake Como. I saw: what it was.

THE SOUFFLÉ

Honey protocols! Hear how they mock: You'll now do nothing at all.
As if a steeped consciousness (sated like a sponge) were refusing
the groundwork. I can't make myself understood. Let's try it like this:
you invite people to eat, at eight, and there lies raw meat, a mound
of flour, dirty carrots and a dozen eggs and you say: That's the soufflé,
if you see what I mean, or if it wasn't *now* but three hours from now,
or if I was someone else, then exactly this here would be: the soufflé.
Your guests ask, more worried than disappointed: So what happened?
What was it that you were doing while you were not making a soufflé?
Oh woe! The sadness of refusal that blames the squandering on itself
and on the squanderers. Because the squanderers squander their care,
they're squandering? Themselves! So much for preanalytical laying about,
which is also no solution here. It's either murky or pure. As you see fit.
Or better: depending what you're after. Looked at like this, the pure is also
murky, very murky. And it murkily insists on the rightness of the pure.
But the guests are right when they say: That's not what a soufflé looks like.

GERMS

Honey protocols! Hear how they mock: Fear no more now!
Hell yeah, let complex fissures effloresce, let germ beget germ
five hundred thousand times. A labial Luna Park of proliferation.
Bring it on, let them form white spots of froth, all over the place,
and embroider stuff – while I'm out cold and you are likewise –
all round the inflammation. Let them interweave what we die of
and what we live off, let them court each other, like bashful fiancés
who've yet to take possession, who bring each other down. Let them
just come. Let them give us another twenty days, let them eat
us from the inside, until we resonate. You clearly don't know yet.
If you knew, you'd be blooming, blossoming with me like algae.

WANT

Honey protocols! Hear how they mock? Now she wants to be very tender with everyone, she also wants to be tender with grammar. She wants to learn everything, to practice, to be one of the people who does everything and never for anything but mercy. She wants to be nice to everyone. She wants to make big eyes and to always say: But it's nicely arranged, just like that, in the nicest possible way, and gladly, of course, yes – but, yes, naturally – and say: But that also has to do with easing the burden, wants to say: Yes, but, that's the structure, and say: Yes, but you're forgetting the effort you've already, and so on and so forth, then she wants to see eyes that brighten, then she wants to see pleasure and she wants to photo-absent herself in it, then she wants precisely this submission to give her back an equivalent of its received tenderness and not the acquiescence, not the distance, neither in space nor in time.

THEORY OF AFFECT

Honey protocols! Hear how they mock: You can't just flatly go in here, as raw as you like. That's odd, I can't hear you at all, due to my screaming, presumably. I wear my wrath as antlers. The rooms where beauty was I've flooded waist-deep in broth, I've overblown the flute, the posthorn, the mouthpiece burst my lips. I raged, I rage. I smoked, I smoke. I sing, make jokes, kiss, sleep. I stared and I stare into the white. I've songs in me and a scythe. Here comes a chopper, says the scythe. And the wrecked village looks darker and clearer. Through the pit of my soul wanders a herd. Where's the flute then? I don't know. The prepleased cattle graze on rotten pastures of yukky clover. Tomorrow is self-slaughtering, skinning, deboning, preserving, proclaims the scythe. No one believes it, though no one objects. This is the idyll turned upside down, sullied from top to bottom. It seems the end of grace has come. And here I must conclude. Yours, with warmest regards, Miss Dynamite. *Watch me explode.*

ROUND WORLD

Honey protocols! Hear how they mock? Sugar-sweet, here
you have it, your round world. Who said that? The dervish.
His horns drilled it open, during training. Turning, borders
whirl over borders, whirl over Libya. Under the auspices.
We go over the top. This upright surface, what'll we call it?
Wall? Or Tortureland? Always glad to oblige, son of the desert.
Expressive conduct: *I'm dying.* Where you doing it? *At home.*
Instrumental conduct: *Stay where you're dying until you're
no longer doing so.* We'll help you in our way, economically.
Long term. Presence. Obligation. Paris-Dakar. Dakar-Paris.
That's the round world, *sans frontières*. Hold on, so they're all
going to live with you now, or what? Be clear: injustice exists.
You embody it and it embodies you. Let that at least be clear.

MONEY

The pure scorn of solvent honey protocols: Listen, it's expensive time, the time that enters where no money is, where things face each other in silence, being fully present unto themselves. But what measure do I use to compare them? The time it takes to understand them, until they start to talk, to sing. The word is one I know, for sure, but can I afford it? I scrimped and saved my breath for it. I said: the commodity expresses the alienation inherent in selling. Back then we distinguished debts from gifts. A distinction we no longer make. We've got time. Loads of time. And we're hungry. If you like my song, give me a chunk of meat from your plate, and put snow in my wine. Like for everyone else. These matters must be ventured, uttered. No one's mentioned venture capital yet. That would be an invert world where money changes one thing into another, virtue to vice, vexation to profit. The incomparability of song and meat converges in me. So am I the great transformer? No, I'm just the end of no time, for now.

BOOZING

Honey protocols! Hear how they mock? They've written everything down!
By using the protocols, whatever took place – or didn't take place! –
can be reconstructed, adapted for the big stage, at any time. So:
You were the one who started it after all! And in the end I was game
for all manner of dalliance! By then, though, there was no one at my side.
Thus did I herdishly dally alone, in the muddled midfield of courtship,
to the detached tones of the shawm, saw the herdsman & the herdsman
get undressed and somewhat later get dressed again. Both were not me.
And then I drank. Yes. Not a lot. Quite a lot. Line by line, Easter-like.
Anacreontics. Boozing for meaning. Is there anything left to drink?
Nail varnish remover. And half a bottle of *Aqua Allegoria* by Guerlain,
plus something luridly yellow from Einsiedeln Abbey, Canton of Schwyz.
Yes, I know, Kierkegaard taught us, not just him, the protocols have all
taught us how pointless it is in the case of such delicate undertakings
to call on the world to repeat itself. Were I to stand, with my sword,
valiantly, in my underwear, the world would surely choose The Silver Gun,
which isn't fair, for our duel. If it's like that I'd rather just let it rest, world,
the next round's on me, I've got the money, and the dregs are yours.

SHELLFISH

Honey protocols! Hear how they mock? Here's a monstrous painting of harvest customs on some distant planet. At the picture's edge, bottom left, there's me as a diver. Wearing gloves that end in hooves instead of hands. How beseeching my hoof strike, my outstretched hand. Whirlwinds fling pieces of ripe fruit aloft, up into red-ringletted skies, and place them, arranged by size, onto sheets of water, through which they immediately sink. I dive to fetch them. Involved in this: shellfish, not the fish as a whole, just its two eyes. Which we use, in the evening, to gaze into the harvest fire, laid back on a slope, on grass, first damp then black. Sorrow, beauty, quiet simplicity, like in a cheap novelette. Turn the pages for me, will you?, I ask the shellfish, who's all eyes and can't do it. Help me – forgetting all about the shellfish I turn to unknown – help me out of this picture, because I can't do it on my own. I'm calling you! But you don't know who you are, damn it. You ought to learn this from me, while on the distant planet harvest customs run their course, the light masses in the red fruits, flailing at them, while light accentuates the blue fruits, dragging them from far to near and bursting them. The sky's afroth! But I'm here, at the mercy of what I can only do alone. And there are days when I can't do even that.

BEGAT

Honey protocols! Hear how they mock? They have an evil hunch. *Is there anything like bad intuition,* I asked and Prof. Hawkey said (quizzically): *Jealousy?* Inneresting, very inneresting. Proceeded to set forth this idea – a picnic rug for us all in our sunlit heyday. For all of us who were still there. In that July of record rainfalls, as you'll recall. Is anyone actually even still there? As if intuition had lost its innocence for ever, all data now unclean, raining down on my parade. Did someone just say palanquin? No? What a pity. One may assume wholescale outdoing of my reasons for precisely the wrong reasons, categorical error, false derivation, and in bed a celebration of same. Denying aggression's undignified. Or can be. The neighbours are fucking. Seems everyone's at it. Jealousy was deletion by mirroring. In this farce not, me not, mirrored in it not, longer want, me. We want to mirror me in this farce no longer. I'm afraid this was jealousy. Such thinking was a curse. For this alone we deserved torment, distress, a good beating. As if one were duty bound to own and carry off what didn't previously exist as property. Such was the rub: jealousy begat property where none was before.

KALOKAGATHIA

Honey protocols! Hear how they mock: The beautiful soul's feeling bad. Ah, if it didn't know itself, it'd feel better. We wave: goodbye subjectivity! The collapse of the faculties put an end to the idea of the beautiful soul that's denied self-realization. If it doesn't self-realize, it may be beautiful, but it's unconscious to me. If it does realize itself, it's no longer beautiful. Ha, what a mockery: I'm no longer the master of my own senses, maybe I never have been. But that really doesn't matter. Ravishing Grace cares little for those she ravishes. *Au contraire*, she goes right along with them down into the abyss, where she then tampers with the interested parties. *Tua res agitur.* If your neighbour's on fire, it's absolutely your business. Grace couldn't care less right now. Instead: mute, unyielding dalliance. You know what, we'll just expurgate her. We'll name our central affect: dissipation, and we'll say: yes. In disenchantment, it would all be clear. To see. What hurt. What didn't. What was all the more painful as a result. Kneel down. But you kneel powerless vis-à-vis. In the steel encasement. Of the disenchanted world. You without panties. With your realized soul. With the broken fan. With the money all blown. *And now, all together, damn it:* The steel encasement. The disenchanted world. The broken fan. All of us without panties. Souls realized in beauty. Blow all the money!

KALOKAGATHIA (carnival song)

63

END-OF

Honey protocols! Hear how they mock? They want to be forward-looking. They're fed up with always just describing what's happened. They want to get out there themselves. Hey, listen, I've got the cash, fifty frikkin euros, and plenty more where that came from. I'll pick you up in a taxi. Tell me the number. I'll be right there. You've got about ten minutes to smarten yourself up. I want to see charm. Windblown hair, wafting into the future. I want to go there. With you. Where? Whatcha mean where?? We don't know yet. We can't know yet, because that, sweetie, is what future is. Obvs. I'll take you there. That's the whole point, the rest is end-of. Look: I can't give you freedom, all I can do is to let you be free. The same way I can't perish someone, all I can do is to let them perish. Yeah, sure, I could give them something to eat. You're absolutely right. But now it's just a matter of you taking what I'm presumably in a position to give you. I'm hanging up now, I'm coming over, I'll take you there.

DAY'S DEBRIS

Honey protocols! Hear how they mock? They were the last to leave. Gimme refill! And why? Because we're darlings, that's why. Refill it with day's debris. The dream of the ingrate party guests lasts ages, a whole decade. Initially we feared their staying away. Later it was them we feared. Round things, the best, gone before the party began, eaten by someone. The guests found the queen's blue outfit too wide, but those who slipped it on began to produce loud talk that everyone had to obey, in silence. The summer in which we slowly submerged was followed by one in which the lamp submerged, and lastly one that submerged itself. Everything was wet. Puddling. Howling wind. Missy Elliott said she'd come. Oh, that made for chafing anticipation and one more letdown. People were cutting themselves into slices. Someone brought a multi-tiered roast but then went astray for years in the staircase. The staircase was big, very big, like in a palace or an embassy. There was an orchestra, on which the guests, no sooner had it started to play, all turned their backs. That was impolite of them to show their backs and make like molecules. The orchestra played in a pit, or rather a trench, a defensive structure. From the little bridge I was standing on I could only wave. Taoist notes became important but were only visible to those passing slowly through the ceiling or through the floor on the paternoster. I took at least four rides, but sadly I can't recall a thing. A dangerous man arrived with a naked, angular dog, but once his angular dog had taken a liking to another of its kind, the dangerous man showed his conciliatory side. That just about worked out, which means: What didn't work out hid somewhere else. Quick, get seeking! As I tried to record the wind, the device cried. Out. With pain. Leave early, leave late. Don't leave at all. See the wings. Seen the wings? Gotta leave! But the ingrate party guests are still here.

SONG OF THE INGRATE PARTY GUESTS

GAMBLING

Honey protocols! Hear how they mock: You can hold or fold.
Bear in mind, you could always just leave. Coat-tails of delight,
let them fly. The stakes are doubled. Meaning something else
is halved? Wait, I'll fill in the players. How many should I put?
I'll write the cards, I'll write the Colts, too. The furrowed brows,
the green baize. The blank, impassive eyes. No one shouts.
Does someone snort? Whenever anyone's to snort, I'll write it.
Hold or fold? Is there not some third option? Stay a little longer
at my side. Royal flush. Straight flush. Something with same
colour pairs. What's on the table now? Hold or fold? What lies
between the two? Disquietment by friendship that always goes
not to the spot where I loved, but to the other table. I could also
decline morally while rising in my own esteem. Unless, that is,
the stakes are doubling again. They are. They're quadrupling.
My friend, as we're about to turn our backs on this here casino,
let's give ourselves new rules. Rule the first: *Wishes are not truth*.

EQUILIBRIUM

Honey protocols! Hear how they mock: That's the unstable equilibrium. Everyone's at risk. Everyone's unstable. The aggressor's unstable and the victim. The one who wasn't there and the one who's joining us later and the one who left early. The harasser's unstable. The one who stopped and the one who started over. The publisher's unstable. Doesn't call back. I'm unstable, too. I wouldn't even answer. The vomitous rabble is unstable. We could call it by some other name, but unfortunately we're too unstable. The unstable are unstable. Hence at risk. The classic bay window's at risk. Along with uncongested road traffic as a whole. Anyone seriously considering self-sacrifice is unstable. We say to him or her: from here on in, self-sacrifice only on condition of voluntariness. After all, we're dealing here with mammals that never simply desire or detest. Instead, their desiring and their detesting must always be willed, too. Which is why they're always so unstable. Hence the cognitive dissonance and the never wholly cured ignorance. Love, what's that like? Unstable. The weather's unstable. Like us, unstable in equilibrium.

FUR

Honey protocols! Hear how they mock? Now we come to the phallus. Or the place where it used to be. Never was. Will grow back some day. Where its ghost dwells. It's not the crotch. No, it's the south of France. Or some other region that means the same. The same due to the loss. The regions clothed in pale fur. Ayee! At this juncture, the fur marks the really truly very last moment when I could possibly give credence to the bloody marvellous idea of the phallic woman. The last tavern before the border that is the fetish. The fetish is the border. Within it an ailing completeness phantasmatically flickers, having already made contact with loss, before everything dissolves into millions of tiny hairs. Meanwhile, however, we know that neither the woman nor the man possesses a penis. Thanks be to Californian academics. The fetishes begin to move. Implosions of melancholy. I get a third arm, it grows out of the basket in which I burrow my beauty, it grows into you. By you here, I mean everybody. It, by which I mean the arm again, covers itself with fur in order to be a desire that's full-bloodedly excited about the loss. It wants to embrace, needs a second. *Strangeness.* Stroking. As if we came from *borderline* to *border collie*, from there to *sauce béarnaise,* and then, at Credence Tavern, supped on *steak-frites*.

WHO WHO WHO

The honey protocols are off duty. But we're giants. We're hysterics.
We're hysterical giants sucking each other's heads dry. Really?
In equal measure? Mine somehow feels like its been sucked drier.
And tell me: We're how many? How many giants? Where do we live?
Have we got a job? Do we beg? Are the gifts we get not far too small
for us because we're giants? And sated – have we ever been that?
When I starve, is it your odyssey that's the reason for that? Is it me?
Who's the source of our obligation? The object of our fiery inclination?
We say: My ancient loverman! My ancient mistress! We giggle: tee-hee.
We've upended ourselves onto our bottlenecks and senseless all else
seems to me. Oh hi! The chaotic mega-fear. Ideals and dosage. *Alas!*
And no one, not one, to record and interpret it for us. Giants we are,
without meaning, seeking the world's best hermeneutician in the world.

SCENT

Honey protocols! Hear how they mock? It's possible that a scent,
a beguiling scent that had me shy with delight as I passed through,
spicy, like the scent of well groomed, giddily fast horses, a scent
in which affection and upheaval raptly propped each other up,
that such a scent will one day be broken down into its elements
(one will be resin, another mossy rot, and a third stiff like acid)
which, thus isolated, will each become drier, cruder, dafter, duller.
Like desire when it points to its unlovely flipside, like laundry
that's done in stagnant water, or an already waterlogged boat,
no longer manoeuvrable, that foolishly tried to pass the rapids
and overturned, overturns! Yes, these are old reflexes. They date
from the days when we had the brains of reptiles. How is reason
supposed to cope with that? Like hurrying on far ahead in order
to repair something that lies far back in primal times. Ah, memory!
What's been broken up remembers its intact self, Lucretius writes,
and therefore smells stronger. What's been pulverized or thoroughly
destroyed by fire. And the same applies here. We cannot go back.

SHADE PLANTS

Wielding a scissor jack you run in among the shade plants.
You batter the light out of them as if it were black honey.
Under the plants, you expose it. They harbour it. The plants
are woodlice. We, too, are woodlice. But this is not our night.
It's just a very long tunnel. A tunnel twenty hours in length.
I'll teach you to frisk deepest darkness – with scissor jacks.
Your body lowers its lids. In behind them, something lilac-like?
Am I mistaken? I'll tell you what my latest impressions are:
bright, lightless, eclipsed, lavender, sense of unadorned you.
All's still deep black. The close-fitting density of outer space.
Then long sleep side by side. Peek-a-boo, gymnast, darkling.
I bet you're dreaming of a tunnel. Or the scent of lavender,
for twenty hours, roughly. Longer the tunnel than the night.
Help yourself. Here's pitch-black *nougat blanc de Montélimar*.
Still unsure whether to run or to wait, whether tunnel or night.

HAYDN

Level with the calyx, I catch a hint of almond. In its insides, the blossom
senses the future. The blossom learns the verbs: to become and to decay.
The blossom's beautiful. Beauty stands bent over in the deep mezzanine,
but what's it waiting for? It's a he, by the way, young as jasmine (she is).
His throat a funicular into the red of dawn. (It used to run through the night,
of course, passages.) Mountain dwellers. Herds of richly decorated beasts.
The Alps were glowing terribly. I don't ask nothing from this scene, I'm just
very tired. Haydn knocks at my door, which he need not do, since he has
the key. He has keys for everything, he has doors for everything. Blossoms.
He arranges the blossoms in a blood-smeared bodice. Haydn rejects this.
He fetches beauty from the mezzanine, unbends it, draws it skywards,
sets its (or his, as we have learned) skull crown upright, towards the skies.
Like everyone's standing on thin air. Haydn's taught us how beautiful this is.

POPLARS

Dwarf rabbit, your ardour! Dwarf rabbit, game for something or other
that mustn't be death. Determination, we're still sitting, in summer,
in the shade of the trees, looking at other trees, shimmering sky.
Thrice the spirits billow out (spirit hair, spirit rivers, spirit virtues).
Thrice we order woodruff shandygaff. By the bowlful. Bowls empty.
Now the poplars can talk, at last, they talk about twinkle machines.
A topic of great interest, to poplars in particular. Nice and silly, yes,
but also nice. And a cocktail of maple syrup, linden blossom, vodka
and elderflower soda, balanced on foreheads down boulevards.
Dwarf rabbit, you reflector of my soul! In billows we shed our guises
and reveal ourselves in all our bright ardour. Driving trucks through
the sluice, our load is tons of stuff that might come in useful because,
as we said, we're game for something or other that mustn't be death.
In billows we're thrilled by the hair, by the rivers, even by the virtues,
and by the poplars' talk of twinkling. Thrilling even to what we lack.
Flutes of champagne brought to us spill-free in the scent of the linden.

SOLITARY SOBBING

Think I'm neglected, where all I meet with are voices,
songs for hire, everyone has their thing. Meseems I
don't. My waist stands around, my legs stand around,
I have to hold myself, there's nothing else that holds me.
I cry all on my own, too. Solitary sobbing's not my thing.
In the morning I stroke the soft toy, in the evening I stroke
the soft toy, it's a grim-faced skinny little horse and me,
I feel shame under its gaze. Its eyes have worked loose,
over all the years, so that its gaze is constantly changing
from morning to evening, sometimes attentive and mild,
but mostly it has more of a grim look. Then I feel shame.
I lie down. I get up again. Solitary sobbing's not my thing.

I LIE DOWN (canon for four voices)

ATLAS

What an inside-out Atlas I am. I stand tottering beneath the globe, spreading degrees of longitude like veils, crazy Atlas that I am. They're your veils, your benediction, your very special cult. As Atlas I labour under myself as I do under the world. But if I gave myself away, would I get myself back intact? Or with pangs in my lungs? See, I want myself no more. Barbarian: me again. What falls so deep is mostly heavy. What flies so far has either wings or jets. What falls so knottily falls deeper, softer, into bed, into the roots of the rootless tree, the dream, the spume, the pudendum, the boat. Stoats are nervous animals, and so are humans. Which turns out favourably for the species. Mirror me beyond recognition, give me back to myself in bits. Nothing, start nothing. Go on doing a thing whose present monstrously lies in a future that's not made and that's blind. *Bone de Chine*. Do understand: I smashed it to piece it back together. The picture's at a slant. The darkness is part of it. Realize: Where it's dark we oughtn't align ourselves with light alone. And should the freshly formed ego wish to be crossed out at long last, it's not allowed. We're against saying yes to darkness in all respects. Consolation for the fully formed ego: you'll live because I'll deform you.

DIVA AND DEALER

Dealer! The diva flings pewter plates. Coolly honours her impotence.
Stage lightning, oops, the turban goes up in feathers or flames.
And out steps: her unborn child, her conscience, her pedigree bitch,
her flokati-clad sex provider, her perfectly turned out horsey boy.
A son of danger, mightily winged, he hurtles off, abroad and aloft.
Hinges at close to full stretch. That's how open the diva was then.
Drug money as ammunition. But dealers quibble. How so? The diva
accuses the dealer of many things, e.g. indolence. Says he rots
away in crime. Pretends to be a bison but is really a calf, or calves.
Says she'll drive stakes into his hippy shit. Says he delivers not
a jot, to either of them. Loser! Next to him, she says, she's seas,
in the plural!!!!! Deduction here is based on free-flowing variables.
The dealer rages like a ram or a sitting boss or a generator, woah!
His free-flowing variable dries up on her touchstone. Glow, worm!
Hereby has the relationship between the sexes been described
with due vigor and in every respect. Now, people, please cast it off.

TRAP

I'm looking into some kind of puppet eyes. Embodiment's a wire cage.
A husk, first stuffed, then washed up, where the plunge pool begins
to go properly pear-shaped. Grow! Grow! Otherwise the scenario
would become entirely improbable. And the reader doesn't like that.
Readers like the lumbar rack. To be thoroughly stretched on the verse.
So that they grin and moan. Maybe even sexually? But no. Not that.
Kittens result in? They don't result. Kittens are the coinage I use
to purchase cement. Oh! Will the reader buy that? Disaster looms.
Cue thunder. Er, thunder looms: cue disaster. Magpie wings spread.
Magpies look. Magpies swell. Magpies grow. Their white parts grow.
Flying past, they bear whole limbs in their beaks. I saw it clear as day.
But for the reader it's not enough. Meanwhile comfy visitors babbled.
Only I read the prophecy. Well, me and the reader read it. It's old,
as old as horsetails (roughly 375 million years). Puppet eyes twitch.
The reader looks into a cluttered, shadowy vestibule and senses:
Something's not quite right here. Could be a trap. No, I don't like this.

HIVE MIND

On the threshold of the age of busyfication: bees, bees, bees.
They serve us as a symbol. But they also serve as a guard.
For no one gets into the honey chamber who might one day
want out again. Newcomers swear on the hive, he or she.
If she broke her word she'd be plagued by the shrill buzzing
of an invisible bee, audible to no one but her. We believe it
to be red. It develops parthogenetically out of the false oath.
Other bees disguise themselves as hum or whistle, as aircon,
tinnitus, flautist, radio mast, secret service, fan, "overtones".
Pass their scant time with atmospheric psychological thrillers,
horror films. In their favourite, my rescue rope becomes a snake.
I sever its head and then fall endlessly downwards. AAAAAH!
Unless swarming bees, all of a sudden, catch me and carry
me safely home. Sudden bee swarms are evidence of what?
Gangs. Perdition. Intact ecosystems. The dazzling bridal bed
of summer's sky. A devalued present. One right answer only.

DRIVING PERMIT

Struggle mode: waves of unease and no escape. Followed by fisticuffs with protocol clerks. But how come it's sweet? Obviously, you can no longer quiz the protocol about this. Drunkenness gives tentativeness a good old proletarian bashing. Primness be gone, enough faltering. My pharynx opens into an underground garage, gigantic base instincts park beside my Jaguar. No, no, that's my Hyundai Sonata. In dark blue with canary leather seats. Note: sublimation doesn't exist. But you can drive there. Or take a little helper to foster inner transport. No more driving after that though. The location's fixed. Painful analysis tells. Drinking with men. Or dealing with them. Once again: sublimation doesn't exist. At dusk we raise a glass. Of firefighting water. To our lives. Drinking with men. The location's fixed. All you can do is leave. One day ants will chauffeur us. Many (many!) years from now.

HONEY

Lastly: the protocol of certain gardens' honey-flowing springs. There's the stickiness of inner fixation, a putty that never dries, and unforgettably there are traces of honey on pieces of paper, on windshields, in bags and pockets, under shoes, on fingers, that recall a mishap. The honey protocol of the flight of bees across those blossoms that are just within reach (of the bees). Linden maybe. Or horse chestnut. We come to view the body as the protocol of our lives. Like a tiny flag amid the bees and raging pollen, the question remains: must one not be intelligent to be capable of such great acts of folly? These glorious songs are not writ by conscious reason. The ones gather for the others, none for themselves alone. The honey stomach is everyone's stomach. The love is everyone's love. Oyez! They who come unstuck inside – will be rescued. Unstuck outside – consumed.

www.ingramcontent.com/pod-product-compliance
Lightning Source LLC
Chambersburg PA
CBHW051607170426
43196CB00040B/2974